W9-BVN-161

I Can Ride a Bike

By Edana Eckart

Welcome Books

Children's Press®
A Division of Scholastic Inc.
New York / Toronto / London / Auckland / Sydney
Mexico City / New Delhi / Hong Kong
Danbury, Connecticut

Photo Credits: Cover and all photos by Maura B. McConnell
Contributing Editor: Jennifer Silate
Book Design: Christopher Logan

Library of Congress Cataloging-in-Publication Data

Eckart, Edana.
I can ride a bike / by Edana Eckart.
        p. cm. — (Sports)
    Includes bibliographical references (p.) and index.
    Summary: When a boy and his mother go cycling together, he shows how to ride correctly and safely.
        ISBN 0-516-23967-8 (lib. bdg.) — ISBN 0-516-24032-3 (pbk.)
        1. Cycling—Juvenile literature. [1. Bicycles and bicycling.] I. Title.

GV1043.5 .E35 2002
796.6'028'9—dc21

                                                                    2001052976

Contents

My name is Tim.

Mom and I are going on a bike ride.

5

I put a bottle of water
on my bike.

I will drink it when
I get **thirsty**.

We put on our **helmets** before we go.

My helmet will keep my head safe if I fall.

I get on my bike.

I put one foot on a **pedal**.

I also hold on to
the **handlebars**.

I push down on the pedals.

I am riding my bike!

The **brakes** are on the handlebars.

I press them when I want to stop.

15

My bike also has a bell.

I ring the bell when we are behind other people.

The people move over
to let us pass.

I want to ride my bike all day.

Bike riding is fun!

New Words

brakes (**brayks**) things that slow down or stop a bike

handlebars (**han**-duhl-barz) the bar at the front of a bike that is used for steering

helmets (**hel**-mits) hard hats that protect people's heads

pedal (**ped**-uhl) a lever that is pushed with the foot to make a bike move

thirsty (**thur**-stee) needing something to drink

To Find Out More

Books
Bicycle Safety
by Nancy Loewen
The Child's World

Let's Find Out About Bicycles
by Mary Ebeltoft Reid
Scholastic Trade

Web Site
The National Highway Traffic Safety Administration's Safety City Bike Tour
http://www.nhtsa.dot.gov/kids/biketour/index.html
Learn about biking and roadway safety on this Web site.

Index

About the Author
Edana Eckart has written several children's books. She enjoys bike riding with her family.

Reading Consultants
Kris Flynn, Coordinator, Small School District Literacy, The San Diego County Office of Education

Shelly Forys, Certified Reading Recovery Specialist, W.J. Zahnow Elementary School, Waterloo, IL

Sue McAdams, Former President of the North Texas Reading Council of the IRA, and Early Literacy Consultant, Dallas, TX